REPORT TO THE CONGRESS

Use of Currency Transaction Reports

Submitted by the

Financial Crimes Enforcement Network

On behalf of the

U.S. Department of the Treasury

October 2002

I. Executive Summary

On October 26, 2001, the President of the United States signed into law the Uniting and Strengthening America by Providing Appropriate Tools Required to Intercept and Obstruct Terrorism (USA PATRIOT ACT) Act of 2001, Public Law 107-56. Section 366 of the USA PATRIOT ACT requires the Secretary of the Treasury to conduct a study regarding the system for exempting bank customers from currency transaction reporting under 31 U.S.C. 5313. The study must consider:

(A) the possible expansion of the statutory exemption system in effect under section 5313 of title 31, United States Code; and

(B) methods for improving financial institution utilization of the statutory exemption provisions as a way of reducing the submission of currency transaction reports that have little or no value for law enforcement purposes, including improvements in the systems in effect at financial institutions for regular review of the exemption procedures used at the institution and the training of personnel in its effective use.

The Secretary of the Treasury submits this report in accordance with the above requirement. The Financial Crimes Enforcement Network ("FinCEN") was directed by the Secretary to carry out the study required by Section 366 because of its regulatory authority over currency transaction reporting under the Bank Secrecy Act ("BSA") and its role in administering the BSA database of which currency transaction reports ("CTRs") form a part.

Methodology

FinCEN's study focused on determining the extent to which depository institutions are using exemptions, identifying the areas in which exemptions are not being used, and the reasons for their lack of use. To make these determinations, FinCEN relied on: (1) a study of the BSA database by its analysts of the categories of exemptible customers for which CTRs were being filed; (2) a survey conducted by a contractor of a random sample of depository institutions concerning, in part, their exemption practices and the reasons underlying them; and (3) an analysis of the exemption process to determine how it could be improved.

Findings

The number of CTRs filed on an annual basis is still extremely high – 12.3 million in FY2002 (although this represents a decrease from the 13 million filed in FY2000). While the number of exemptions that have been filed with FinCEN has increased substantially since FinCEN's phase-in of the current exemption process was completed in 2000, the 118,678 exemptions filed in FY 2002 represent only a tiny fraction of total CTR filings. Many financial institutions have taken advantage of exemptions for government entities, educational institutions and utilities, but financial institutions generally have not taken advantage of exemptions for large companies that either have a cash intensive business or are payroll customers. Some financial institutions are not taking advantage of the exemption process at all; for example, for small institutions that do not file many CTRs, exemptions do not appear to be cost effective.

The most frequently cited reasons by survey respondents for not using the exemption system were:

- The fear of regulatory action if an exemption turns out to be wrong;

- Difficulty in determining whether a customer is eligible for exemption;

- The additional costs associated with due diligence;

- Lack of staff time to review CTRs for possible exemptions; and

- The transactions requiring CTR filings are too infrequent.[1]

Recommendations

Based on these findings, the Secretary offers the following recommendations for legislative and/or regulatory change.

- FinCEN should work with the federal bank regulators, as well as banks, to reduce, as appropriate, fear of adverse regulatory consequences from making incorrect exemption determinations, including issuing an Advisory encouraging the use of the exemption process.

- FinCEN, in conjunction with the federal bank regulators, should draft and disseminate a new exemption handbook with a view to making the exemption system easier for bank personnel to understand.

- FinCEN should revise the waiting period requirement for non-listed customers to permit banks to use a risk-based approach in determining when to exempt a customer.

- FinCEN should amend the exemption regulation to simplify and make less burdensome the biennial certification and monitoring system requirement for non-listed customers.

- The exemption process should not be made mandatory, nor are any other statutory changes necessary at this time. FinCEN should continue to seek ways to improve the efficiency and efficacy of the CTR reporting system. It should also work toward achieving an accurate measurement of the success of

---

[1] This response reflects the fact that smaller depository institutions, which are less likely to conduct large cash transactions, constituted the majority of depository institutions in the survey, and, in fact, outnumber such large institutions.

the system. These steps will help achieve the goal of finding the optimal balance between the value of the BSA reporting system and database and the burdens imposed to create and maintain it.

II.   CTRs and the Exemption Process

A. Statutory Treatment of CTRs

The Bank Secrecy Act (BSA), codified at 31 U.S.C. 5311 et seq., authorizes the Secretary of the Treasury to issue regulations requiring banks to keep records and file reports that are determined to have a high degree of usefulness in criminal, tax and regulatory matters, or in the conduct of intelligence or counter-intelligence activities, to protect against international terrorism, and to implement anti-money laundering compliance programs and compliance procedures. Regulations implementing the BSA appear at 31 CFR Part 103. The authority to administer the BSA has been delegated to the Director of FinCEN.

The reporting by financial institutions of transactions in currency in excess of $10,000 on Currency Transaction Reports (CTRs) has been the centerpiece of the BSA since its inception. The $10,000 reporting requirement is imposed by a regulation, 31 CFR 103.22, issued under the authority of 31 U.S.C. 5313(a). Until 1996, CTRs were the primary BSA tool used by law enforcement to identify activity indicative of money laundering.[2] Since 1996, when FinCEN and the bank regulators issued final regulations requiring the filing of Suspicious Activity Reports (SARs), SARs have, as expected, replaced CTRs as the primary tool for identifying suspicious activity. CTRs, however, continue to play an important role in law enforcement investigations, following the money trail. For example, an unsuspicious large currency transaction may link what would otherwise appear to be unrelated incidents of suspicious activity. FinCEN analysts performing data mining for proactive case referral also rely on CTRs to track large currency transactions related to persons and accounts identified in SARs. Inquiries made in the BSA database over the past several years have resulted in a significant number of responsive CTRs. For example, in calendar year 2001, there were 1,132,454 queries made into the BSA database, which yielded 1,525,099 responsive CTRs. In other words, for each query made (during which the entire database is searched), an average of more than one CTR responsive to the query was retrieved.

Before the advent of SARs, using CTRs to find indicia of suspicious activity entailed review of individual CTRs. Therefore, the number of CTRs being filed for routine business activity raised concerns about law enforcement's ability to effectively use the database.[3] In response to this concern (as well as concerns of efficiency and cost), the Money Laundering Suppression Act of 1994 (MLSA) amended the BSA by establishing a statutory exemption system for currency transaction reporting.[4] The MSLA established two classes of exemptions:

---

[2] See Money Laundering: A Framework for Understanding U.S. Efforts Overseas (General Accounting Office May 24, 1996).

[3] See id. at 4.1.

[4] Section 402 (b) of the MLSA explained that under the terms of the newly created exemption process, the Secretary was to seek ways to reduce, within a reasonable time, the

Phase I (the so-called mandatory exemptions[5] of Section 5313(d)) and Phase II (the so-called discretionary exemptions of Section 5313(e)).

Under Section 5313(d), Treasury is required, pursuant to regulations, to exempt from the reporting requirements of Section 5313(a) transactions between depository institutions and four specified categories of customers:

1) Another depository institution;

2) A department or agency of the United States, any State or any political subdivision of any State;

3) Any entity established under the laws of the United States, a State, or any political subdivision of any State or under an interstate compact between two or more States, which exercise governmental authority on behalf of the United States or any such State or political subdivision; and

4) Any business or category of business the reports on which have little or no value for law enforcement agencies.

Under section 5313(e)(4)(A) and (B), Treasury is authorized to establish, by regulation, the criteria for granting an exemption process between depository institutions and "qualified business customers." A qualified business customer is defined in the statute to mean a customer that:

1) Maintains a transaction account (as defined in section 19(b)(1)(C) of the Federal Reserve Act) at the depository institution;

2) Frequently engages in transactions with the depository institution that is subject to currency transaction reporting; and

3) Meets criteria that Treasury determines are sufficient to ensure that the purposes of the BSA are carried out without requiring currency transactions reporting with respect to the customer's transactions.

For qualified business customers, section 5313(e)(5) authorizes Treasury to prescribe regulations requiring each depository institution to (A) review, at least once each year, the

---

number of CTRs filed in the aggregate by depository institutions by at least 30 percent in the year preceding the enactment of the MLSA (1994). In drafting these statutory provisions, Congress sought to correct identified deficiencies in the existing administrative exemption system established by Treasury under the general exemptive authority in 31 U.S.C. 5318(a)(6).

[5] The use of the term "mandatory exemption" does not mean that banks are required to exempt these customers but that the availability of the exemption is mandated by statute. Banks are not required to exempt eligible customers regardless of whether they are eligible for exemption under Phase I or Phase II.

qualified business customers of such institution with respect to whom an exemption has been granted under this subsection, and (B) upon the completion of such review, resubmit information about such customers, with such modifications as the institution determines to be appropriate, to Treasury for its approval.

B. The Exemption Regulations

In response to the mandate of the MLSA, FinCEN initiated a rulemaking process relating to the Phase I exemptions of 31 U.S.C.5313(d), which lead to the issuance of an interim rule in 1996. In 1997, FinCEN issued a final Phase I exemption rule and an interim rule for the Phase II exemptions of 31 U.S.C. 5313(e). FinCEN issued a final Phase II exemption rule in 1998. These rules were codified at 31 CFR 103.22(d), and required banks, by October 21, 1998 (in the case of newly granted exemptions) and by July 1, 2000 (for previously granted exemptions) to begin using the new exemption system. The rules establish categories of entities eligible for Phase I and Phase II exemptions (generally banks, governmental entities, public companies, and domestic companies that have cash intensive businesses or payrolls) and a self-executing procedure for banks wishing to take advantage of the exemptions. These procedures require banks to file with FinCEN an exemption form for each customer, and to perform due diligence in making the exemption determinations and in reviewing their continuing appropriateness. In addition, the rules include a safe harbor from BSA civil penalty liability for exemption determinations made in good faith.

Phase I exemptions (31 CFR 103.22 (d)(2)(i)-(v)) apply to the following categories:
- a bank,
- a government agency,
- a government instrumentality,[6]
- a publicly traded business (referred to in the regulations as a "listed business");[7] or
- certain subsidiaries of publicly traded businesses.[8]

---

[6] These three classes of persons—banks, government agencies, and government instrumentalities—are the three classes specifically prescribed by the statute as eligible for a Phase I exemption. Although the regulation uses the term "bank," all depository institutions are within the class of financial institutions that may be exempted under Phase I.

[7] The regulation defines a listed business as any entity, other than a bank, whose common stock or analogous equity interests are listed on the New York Stock Exchange or the American Stock Exchange or whose common stock or analogous equity interests have been designated as a Nasdaq National Market Security listed on the Nasdaq Stock Market (except stock or interests listed under the separate "Nasdaq Small-Cap Issues" heading) provided that, for the purposes of this definition, a person that is a financial institution, other than a bank, is an exempt person only to the extent of its domestic operations.

[8] The regulation defines these eligible subsidiaries as any subsidiary, other than a bank, of any listed business that is organized under the laws of the United States or of any State and at least 51 per cent of whose common stock or analogous equity interest is owned by the listed entity, provided that, for the purposes of this definition a person that is a financial institution, other than a bank, is an exempt person only to the extent of its domestic operations.

A business that does not fall into any of the above categories may still be exempted under the Phase II exemptions (31 CFR 103.22 (d) (2) (vi)-(vii)) if it qualifies as either ‚a "non-listed business" or as a "payroll customer."

A non-listed business is defined as an enterprise that, to the extent of its domestic operations and only with respect to transactions conducted through its exemptible accounts, (i) has maintained a transaction account at the exempting bank for at least 12 months; (ii) frequently engages in transactions in currency with the bank in excess of $10,000; and (iii) is incorporated or organized under the laws of the United States or State, or is registered as and is eligible to do business within the United States or a State. Certain businesses are ineligible to be treated as an exempt non-listed business, (31 CFR 103.22(d)(6)(viii)). An ineligible business is defined as a business engaged primarily in one or more of specified activities.[9] A business that engages in multiple business activities may be treated as a non-listed business so long as no more than 50% of its gross revenues per year are derived from one or more of the ineligible business activities listed in the rule.

A payroll customer is defined solely with respect to withdrawals for payroll purposes from existing exemptible accounts as a person who: (i) has maintained a transaction account at the bank for at least 12 months; (ii) operates a firm that regularly withdraws more than $10,000 in order to pay its United States employees in currency; and (iii) is incorporated or organized under the laws of the United States or a State, or is registered as and is eligible to do business within the United States or a State.

The new rules also established specific procedures for exempting eligible customers. In determining whether to exempt a customer, a bank must take and document such steps as a reasonable and prudent bank would take to protect itself from loan or other fraud or loss based on misidentification of a person's status. The bank must document the basis for its decision to exempt a customer from currency transaction reporting and maintain such documents for five years. After a bank has decided to exempt a customer, the bank must file a Designation of Exempt Person form within 30 days after the first customer transaction the bank wishes to exempt. For Phase I customers, the form has to be filed only once (though the bank must annually review the customer's status). For Phase II customers, the form must be refiled every two years as part of the biennial renewal process. (As with Phase I customers, the bank must also annually review the status of Phase II customers.)

Under the biennial renewal process applicable to Phase II customers, a bank must include

---

[9] Serving as financial institutions or agents for financial institutions of any type; purchase or sale to customers of motor vehicles of any kind, vessels, aircraft, farm equipment or mobile homes; the practice of law, accountancy, or medicine; the auctioning of goods; chartering or operation of ships, buses, or aircraft; pawn brokerage; gaming of any kind (other than licensed pari-mutuel betting at race tracks); investment advisory services or investment banking services; real estate brokerage; title insurance and real estate closings; trade union activities; and any other activity that may, from time to time, be specified by FinCEN.

the following information on the refiled Designation of Exempt Person form: any change in control of the exempt person known to the bank (or for which the bank has reason to know), and a certification regarding the bank's suspicious activity reporting program. In particular, the bank must certify that as part of its annual review of the Phase II customer, the bank has applied as necessary the bank's suspicious transaction monitoring system. While the regulation specifically addresses suspicious activity monitoring in the context of Phase II customers, nothing in the regulation relieves a bank's responsibility for monitoring, as appropriate, suspicious activity in the case of Phase I customers.

The new rules, 31 CFR 103.22(d)(8), include a safe harbor which provides that a bank is not liable for the failure to file a CTR with respect to a transaction in currency by an exempt person, unless the bank knowingly provides false or incomplete information or has reason to believe that the customer does not qualify as an exempt customer.   Absent any specific knowledge or information indicating that a customer no longer meets the requirements of an exempt person, the bank is entitled to a "safe harbor" from civil penalties to the extent it continues to treat that customer as an exempt customer until the date of the customer's annual review.

Under the old system of exemptions, there was no comparable provision protecting financial institutions from liability for erroneous exemption filings made in good faith. Treasury's OFE, and later FinCEN, levied a number of penalties against banks that made erroneous exemption filings. Since the new rules went into effect and were incorporated into FinCEN's enforcement program in 1998, that has changed and FinCEN has limited its enforcement program to willful violations.

III. Trends in CTR and Exemption Filings.

Since 1994, CTR filings have continued to increase, peaking in FY 2000 at 13 million, with slight decreases to 12.6 million in FY 2001 and to 12.3 million in FY 2002 (see Chart 1). As the new exemptions were phased in, beginning with the transitional rules in 1996 and continuing through the effective date of the final rules in July 2000, exemption filings increased from 20,283 in FY 1996 to 68,733+++++++++ in FY 2000, and then to 107,600 in FY 2001 and 118,678 in FY 2002 (see Chart 2). In terms of the percentage of exemptions compared to overall CTR filings, the number of exemptions is miniscule, ranging from .002% (FY 1998) to .01% (FY 2002) on an annual basis.

FinCEN analysts conducted a study of the BSA database to attempt to determine why CTRs continued to rise despite the implementation of the new exemption procedures.   They chose a sample of the CTRs in the database—all CTRs filed for the six-month period that the final exemptions were phased in (January through June 2000)—a total of 6,530,118. This sample was compared to a sample from before the exemption rules went into effect (all CTRs from the first six months of 1995). Review of the sample indicated that there had been a significant drop in the number of CTRs filed in only eight of the approximate 75 occupational categories captured on CTRs. These included transactions by governmental entities (decrease from 81,566 to 7,263 filings); utilities (22,077 to 4,549); educational institutions (4,918 to 1,984); construction/hardware (48,915 to 19,986); transportation (18,624 to 11,595); consumer electronics (19,357 to 7,533); department stores (231,387 to 87,965); and drug stores (82,005 to 26,816). The remaining 67 occupational categories reflected minimal decrease, no change, or an increase in the number of filings. To determine whether significant numbers of CTRs were being filed on other types of entities that could be exempted, the analysts stratified the data to show multiple filings on the same entities during the six-month period. In particular, they looked for instances where more than 150 filings were made on the same entity during the six month period.[10]

The data showed that 1.6 million CTRs were filed on subjects for which 150 or more large currency transactions were reported in the six-month period. This number represents 24% of all CTR filings for that period. The subjects of these CTRs generally were public companies, large regional companies, and franchisees of large companies (e.g., McDonalds). The predominant businesses (63% of total) were retail stores (318,370 or 20%); restaurants/fast food (275,365 or 18%); convenience/gasoline (252,399 or 16%); and retail grocery (142,594 or 9%). The majority appears to be exemptible under either Phase 1 (public company) or Phase 2 (non-listed business incorporated in or doing business in the United States with transaction account for 12 months that frequently engages in large currency transactions or regularly withdraws more than $10,000 to pay its U.S. employees in currency.)

The study also looked at the financial institutions responsible for the greatest number of multiple CTR filings. All of them were national banks with multiple branch offices. The top 20 banks (those with the greatest number of customers on which more than 150 CTRs were filed) were responsible for approximately 43% of such CTRs. The total number of exemptions ever filed by these banks ranged from a low of 3 to a high of 2,987. Only five of these banks had filed over 1,000 exemptions. The low filers appear to be bypassing the exemption process in total. Even those banks with the greatest numbers of exemption filings were exempting no more than 12% of exemptible customers.

The study, together with FinCEN's analysis of the exemption process, has led to the following conclusions:

- Although many financial institutions have taken advantage of the exemptions for government entities, educational institutions and utilities—which are the easiest exemptions to apply—some financial institutions are simply bypassing the entire exemption process;

- There have been relatively few significant decreases in CTR filings on transactions by large companies that have either a cash-intensive business or payroll operations; and

- Financial institutions through which these repeat transactions are conducted are in the best position to determine whether the transactions are exemptible.

IV. Contractor Study.

---

[10] A threshold of 150 + multiple filings per six-month period was set because data sets generated at lower thresholds were too large to be manipulated by FinCEN analysts.

To determine the reasons that depository institutions file CTRs on customers that are eligible for exemption, FinCEN hired a contractor to perform a study in which a group of financial institutions would be surveyed on their use of the exemption system (the "Contractor Study").[11] Working with several federal regulatory agencies, national trade associations, and financial institution compliance officers, the Contractor developed a survey instrument. (See Appendix B.) The Office of Management and Budget approved the survey instrument.

The population of depository institutions to which the survey instrument would be distributed was determined by stratifying a comprehensive list of U.S. banks, savings and loans and credit unions by type of institution and asset size in order to ensure that a random sample would include a range of financial institutions. Banks were divided into the following stratum: (a) Small Banks (less than $55 million in assets); (b) Medium Banks (between $55 and $145 million in assets); (c) Large Banks (between $145 million to $32 billion in assets); and (d) Mega Banks (more than $32 billion in assets). Savings and loans were not divided given their more homogenous nature, as well as the smaller number of institutions from which to sample. Credit Unions were divided into (a) assets between $10 and $32 million and (b) assets in excess of $32 million.

From this list, a number of small, medium, and large banks were selected in approximate proportion to their numbers on the list. All mega banks within the sample were asked to complete the survey, given their small number and the fact that, on average, they file the greatest number of CTRs. The survey was programmed into a website maintained by the contractor, and distributed to 10,606 institutions by electronic mail and fax on August 29, 2002. A total of 2,628 depository institutions, or 24.7% of survey recipients, provided responses to the survey. (See Chart 3.) The contractor determined that this constituted a statistically significant response.

An analysis of the survey results indicates that responses can best be broken down into two categories: responses by mega banks,[12] and responses by all other survey respondents. This reflects many differences between mega banks and all other depository institutions, including the number of customers, and the number of transactions for which CTRs are required to be filed annually at depository institutions falling within each category.

----

[11] The Contractor Study was also designed to collect data that will be used by Treasury for purposes of Objective 1 of Goal 3 of the National Money Laundering Strategy of 2001, which requires Treasury to (1) survey depository institutions to determine the actual costs of currency transaction and suspicious activity reporting requirements, (2) increase usage of the exemption regulations, and (3) survey the financial institutions industry for possible additional categories of CTR filing exemptions. See National Money Laundering Strategy of 2001, Goal 3, Objective 1. For this reason, the scope of the report prepared by the contractor was necessarily greater than the scope of the study required by Section 366. While Treasury intends to use all of the information contained in the Contractor Study, only the information relevant to the requirement contained in Section 366 of the USA PATRIOT Act has been used for this report.

[12] There were 30 mega bank recipients of the survey, and 19 of them provided responses.

The survey asked depository institutions to estimate the percentage of the CTRs that they filed in 2001 on exemptible customers. Among the entire population of survey respondents, 81.2% indicated that they had not filed any CTRs on customers that are eligible for exemption under Phase I of the exemption rules, while 11.5% of the respondents indicated that between 1 and 25% were filed on customers eligible for Phase I exemption. The breakdown of responses by institution size shows that smaller depository institutions are filing a relatively small percentage of CTRs on Phase I eligible customers. However, the responses of mega banks differed considerably from those of the other survey respondents. Among mega banks, 21.1% indicated that they had not filed any CTRs on Phase I eligible customers for 2001, while 57.9% indicated that between 1 and 25% of their CTRs were filed on Phase I eligible customers.[13]

Respondents filed a greater percentage of CTRs on Phase II eligible customers. Among the entire population of survey respondents, 53.8% indicated that they had not filed any CTRs in 2001 on Phase II eligible customers, while 25.9% of respondents indicated that between 1 and 25% were filed on customers eligible for Phase II exemption. Among mega banks responding to the survey, only 10.5% indicated that they had not filed any CTRs on Phase II exemptible customers in 2001. However, 36.8% indicated that between 1 and 25% of CTRs filed in 2001 were filed on Phase II exemptible customers, and 21.1% indicated that between 26 and 50% of CTRs were filed on Phase II eligible customers.[14]

The survey instrument asked recipients to rate twelve possible factors as to their importance in the recipient's decision to file CTRs on customers eligible for exemption. They were asked to rate each factor separately for Phase I and Phase II customers. The factor that elicited the highest overall positive response for both Phase I and Phase II eligible customers was "transactions requiring CTR filings are too infrequent to warrant filing an exemption." This factor should be considerably less important to mega banks, which file the vast majority of all CTRs filed each year.[15]

An additional factor that elicited a high rate of positive response across the strata of survey respondents for both Phase I and Phase II eligible customers was "additional costs associated with conducting due diligence." Respondents cited "fear of regulatory action if an exemption is filed wrongly" as a significant factor in filing CTRs on exemptible Phase I customers, and "difficulty in determining eligibility for exemption" as a significant factor in filing CTRs on exemptible Phase II customers. (See Chart 4.)

The responses provided by mega banks differed from those provided by smaller depository institutions. For mega banks, the three factors that elicited the highest positive

---

[13] However, over one-third (36.8%) of the mega banks did not know what percentage of their customers fell into an exemptible category.

[14] However, 36.8% of these mega banks did not know what percentage of their customers fell into an exemptible category.

[15] The average number of CTRs filed annually by survey respondents with assets under $55 million was 125. Survey respondents with assets between $55 and $145 million file an average of 355 CTRs annually, and those with assets over $145 million file 2,767 CTRs annually. In contrast, mega banks file on average 301,429 CTRs each year.

response to the question why they file CTRs on Phase I eligible customers were: "difficulty in determining eligibility," "additional costs associated with conducting due diligence," and "lack of staff time to review CTRs for possible exemptions." For Phase II eligible customers, mega banks indicated that they file CTRs rather than exempt such customers due to fear of regulatory action for wrongly-filed exemptions, additional costs associated with due diligence, and lack of staff time to review CTRs for possible exemptions, and difficulty in determining eligibility for exemption. (See Chart 5.)

Overall, the following reasons for not using the exemption system received the highest volume of positive responses:

- Transactions requiring CTR filings are too infrequent to warrant filing an exemption.

- Difficulty in determining whether a customer is eligible for exemption.

- Fear of regulatory action if an exemption turns out to be wrong.

- Additional costs associated with due diligence.

- Lack of staff time to review CTRs for possible exemptions.

Thus, the Contractor Survey provided useful insight into both the extent to which depository institutions utilize the exemption system, and their reasons for not doing so to the extent that had been envisioned by Treasury in promulgating that system.

V. Findings and Recommendations for Administrative Action

Many financial institutions have taken advantage of the exemption system to exempt the transactions of customers that are banks and governmental entities – entities that constitute a segment of those customers eligible for exemption under Phase I. However, there has been no significant change in CTR filings on transactions by large companies that have either a cash-intensive business or are payroll customers companies (which may be eligible for exemption under Phase I as public companies and their subsidiaries, or under Phase II as nonlisted entities or payroll customers). Therefore, the following recommendations for administrative action apply to both Phase I and Phase II exemptions.

> **(1) FinCEN should work with the federal bank regulators, as well as banks, to reduce, as appropriate, fear of adverse regulatory consequences from making incorrect exemption determinations.**

Survey responses indicate that depository institutions are hesitant to utilize exemptions out of fear that an improper designation will lead to adverse regulatory action. Thus, FinCEN should work with the bank regulators to determine methods for providing guidance on the types of exemption cases to which the agencies believe civil penalties should apply, and guidance about the protections against liability contained in the exemption rule itself. FinCEN should work with banks in a similar manner to allay their concerns and encourage their use of the exemptions.

There is an inherent tension in the regulatory process between encouraging the use of exemptions and ensuring that they are properly applied. If a bank has an exemption process, that process will be examined; while if it does not, there is nothing to examine, which can create a perverse incentive for banks.[16] Banks are concerned that, even if they are no longer subject to BSA penalties for incorrect exemption determinations made in good faith, they will be cited in ---examination reports for incorrect exemptions. Treasury does not want to discourage bank examiners from undertaking careful reviews to ensure exemption processes at banks are properly applying the exemption criteria; at the same time there should be a policy of encouraging the use of exemptions.[17] Therefore, FinCEN should work with the bank regulators to determine whether the bank examination process can be used to encourage exemptions with an emphasis on the process for establishing an exemption system and making exemption determinations.

(2) FinCEN, in conjunction with the federal bank regulators, should draft and disseminate a new exemption handbook with a view to making the exemption system easier for bank personnel to understand.

A significant number of depository institutions responding to the contractor survey indicated that they believe the exemption procedures of 31 CFR 103.22(d) are difficult to understand and implement. Difficulty in determining whether a customer can properly be exempted leads such entities to choose to file CTRs rather than utilize the exemption system, particularly with respect to non-listed customers. Currently, the only FinCEN guidance on the exemption process is that provided by a FinCEN Advisory published in October, 1998.[18] Respondents indicated that the ability to consult a governmentally-issued exemption handbook would give them substantial incentive to use the exemption process. Therefore, FinCEN, in conjunction with the federal banking regulators, should draft and disseminate a detailed exemption handbook that will better enable financial institutions to understand and utilize the exemption system.

(3) FinCEN should revise the waiting period requirement for non-listed customers to permit banks to use a risk-based approach in determining when to exempt a customer.

---

[16] For example, we reviewed the examination handbook for one agency, which contained procedures for examining the accuracy of the exemption process, but did not contain any procedures for determining whether a bank was filing numerous CTRs on customers eligible for exemption.

[17] As long as exemptions are purely voluntary, a failure to use them cannot be the basis for disciplinary action, but regulators can use the examination process to encourage the use of CTR exemptions and review with the banks how their filings could decrease with proper use of the exemptions.

[18] See FinCEN Advisory Issue 10: Reformed CTR Exemption Process: Questions & Answers (October 1998), available on FinCEN's website at www.fincen.gov.

In order for a bank to exempt a customer as a non-listed business or payroll customer, the customer must have maintained a transaction account with the bank for at least 12 months. See 103.22(d)(2)(vi)(A). The purpose of the 12-month period is to ensure that, prior to exempting a customer, a bank has had sufficient time to become familiar with the frequency and size of a customer's large currency transactions. However, forty-two percent of mega banks and forty-eight percent of the other financial institutions responding to the survey indicated that reducing the length of time before which an exemption may be granted would reduce the burden of using the exemption system.

FinCEN agrees that the 12-month waiting period should not be a minimum requirement. In many instances, (e.g., a department store), the cash intensive nature of a well-established business will be quickly apparent. In other cases, particularly for new businesses, the length of time needed to determine the propriety of exempting a customer may vary. Banks are in the best position to determine the length of time needed to make such judgments about their customers. Indeed, in enacting regulations pursuant to the USA PATRIOT ACT, FinCEN has recognized the importance of permitting banks to make risk-based determinations to accomplish the anti-money laundering requirements with which they must comply.[19] Permitting banks to make a risk-based determination of when to exempt an eligible customer should create an appropriate balance between ensuring that banks are familiar with the transaction activities of their customers, and permitting banks flexibility in making exemptions. Therefore, FinCEN should revise the waiting period requirement for non-listed customers and payroll customers to permit banks to use a risk-based approach in determining when to exempt a customer.

(4) FinCEN should amend the exemption regulation to simplify and make less burdensome the biennial certification and monitoring system requirement for non-listed customers.

Consistent with the statutory mandate,[20] the exemption regulations require banks to review their Phase II exemptions annually. In addition, the regulations specify that banks shall maintain a suspicious transaction monitoring system reasonably designed to detect, for Phase II customers, those transactions in currency that would require a bank to file a suspicious transaction report. Finally, the regulations require banks to refile a Designation of Exempt Person (DEP) form every two years to renew existing Phase II exemptions. The renewal DEP must include the following: information concerning any change in ownership of the Phase II customer, and a certification regarding the bank's suspicious activity reporting program. In particular, banks must certify that as part of their annual review of any Phase II customer, they have applied as necessary their suspicious transaction monitoring system to the customer.[21]

---

[19] See, e.g., Notice of Proposed Rulemaking that would require Customer Identification Program for Banks, Savings Associations, and Credit Unions, 67 FR 48290 (July 23, 2002).

[20] See 31 U.S.C. 5313(e)(5).

[21] The preamble to the final rule indicates that FinCEN did not believe that monitoring and certification would pose additional burdens on banks, because they remain subject in any event to the requirement to file reports of suspicious activity with respect to any transaction they exempt. See 63 FR 50147, 50155 (September 21, 1998).

Nearly three-quarters of mega banks viewed the additional costs associated with continually reviewing exemption eligibility to be an important factor in not exempting all eligible Phase II customers. In addition, according to the survey, the certification language in 31 CFR 103.22(d)(5)(ii) has been interpreted by banks as imposing an obligation beyond the suspicious transaction monitoring and reporting requirement that all banks are subject to regardless of whether a customer is exempted from currency transaction reporting.

The certification process was never intended to impose enhanced due diligence obligations concerning exempted customers. FinCEN, after consultation with its law enforcement partners, should amend the exemption regulation to simplify and make less burdensome the biennial certification and monitoring system for non-listed customers and payroll customers.

(5) The exemption process should not be made mandatory, nor are any other statutory changes necessary at this time.

For institutions that do not file sufficient CTRs to justify the use of the exemption process, making the exemption process mandatory would be particularly burdensome. The exemption process was designed to benefit financial institutions as well as law enforcement. Penalizing financial institutions that do not find it to be a benefit would be inconsistent with this objective. FinCEN believes the system is capable of absorbing excess CTRs in such circumstances, especially since such CTRS do not represent a burden on law enforcement in light of the way CTRs are now used. No statutory changes are necessary at this time.

Conclusion

CTRs provide important information to law enforcement and represent an important and frequently used link in following the money trail. Because the way CTRs are used has changed with the advent of SARs, the law enforcement concerns animating the exemption process no longer exist. Nonetheless, seeking to reduce the number of unnecessary CTR filings is still a valid concern in terms of costs to both the industry and the government. Treasury and FinCEN are committed to seeking ways to improve the system and ensure that regulatory burdens are justified by the benefits of the system.

The recommendations in this report are incremental. They represent feasible measures that can be taken to address the most significant issues identified both by FinCEN's analysis of the database and by the depository institutions responding to the survey questions. The recommendations are aimed at eliminating perceived and actual regulatory disincentives toward use of exemptions, providing better education and guidance about the exemption process, and streamlining the process where possible.

Appendix A

Chart 1

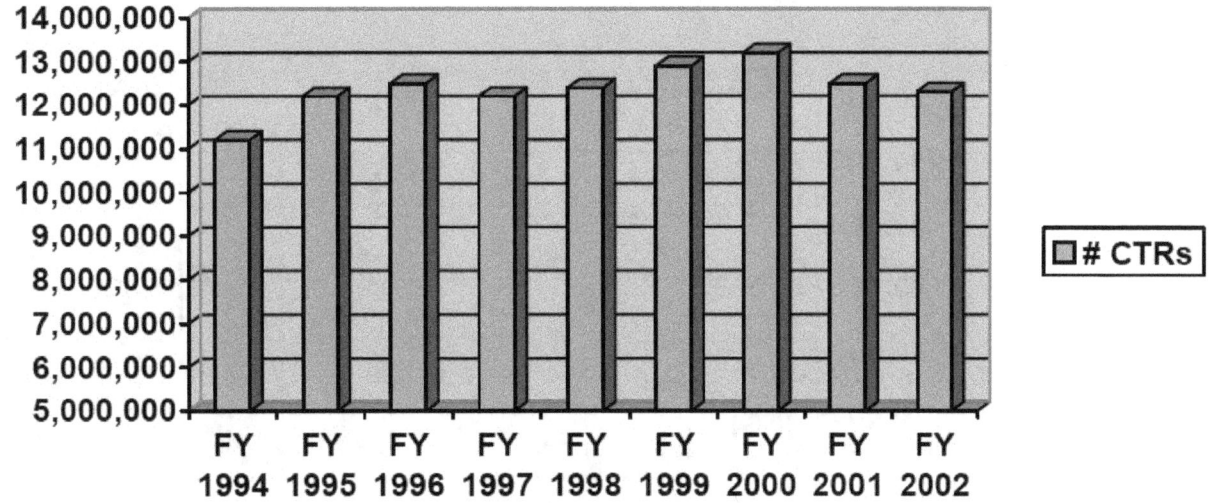

Fiscal Year CTR Filings   FY 1994 – FY 2002

Chart 2

Initial/Biennial Exemptions Filed FY 1996 – FY 2002

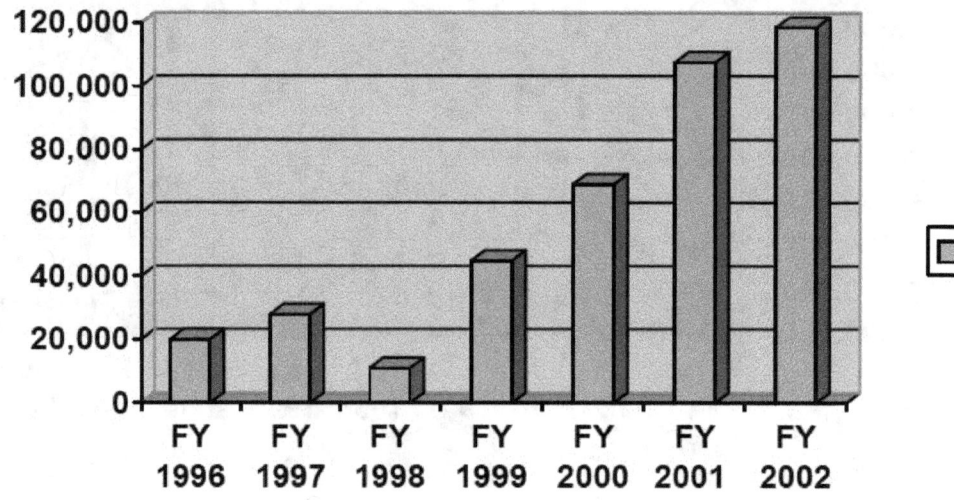

Chart 3

Respondent Counts and Percentages, per Stratum

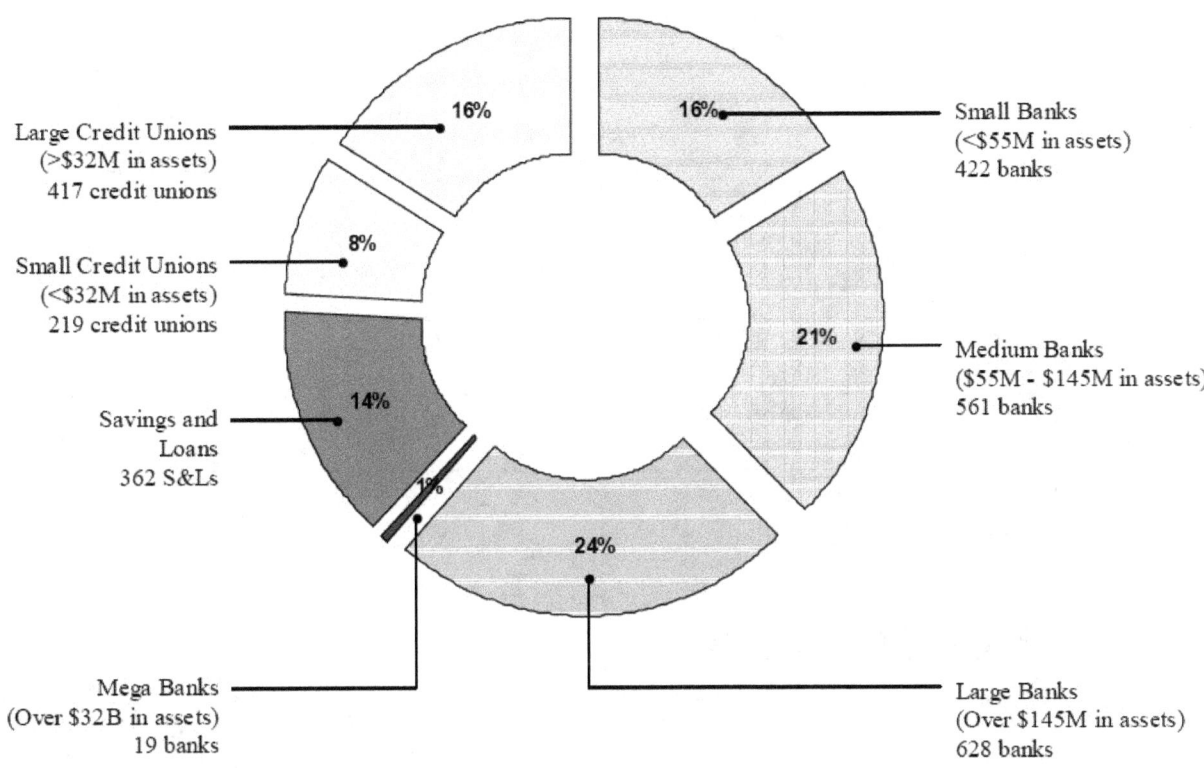

Large Credit Unions
(>$32M in assets)
417 credit unions — 16%

Small Banks
(<$55M in assets)
422 banks — 16%

Small Credit Unions
(<$32M in assets)
219 credit unions — 8%

Medium Banks
($55M - $145M in assets)
561 banks — 21%

Savings and
Loans
362 S&Ls — 14%

Mega Banks
(Over $32B in assets)
19 banks — 1%

Large Banks
(Over $145M in assets)
628 banks — 24%

Chart 4

All Survey Respondents: Top Reasons for Not Exempting all Eligible Phase I and Phase II Customers.

Phase I Customers

Reason	Percentage of Survey Respondents indicating that reason is "important" or "somewhat important" in decision not to exempt all eligible customers
Transactions requiring CTR filings are too infrequent to warrant filing an exemption	33%
Fear of Regulatory Action if an exemption turns out to be wrong	28%
Additional costs associated with conducting due diligence	26%
Difficulty in determining eligibility for exemption	25%
Lack of staff time to review CTRs for possible exemptions	25%

Phase II Customers

Reason	Percentage of Survey Respondents indicating that reason is "important" or "somewhat important" in decision not to exempt all eligible customers
Transactions requiring CTR filings are too infrequent to warrant filing an exemption	41%
Difficulty in determining eligibility for exemption	36%
Fear of Regulatory Action if an exemption turns out to be wrong	35%
Additional costs associated with conducting due diligence	34%

Chart 5

Mega Banks: Importance of Reasons for Not Exempting all Eligible Phase I and Phase II Customers.[22]

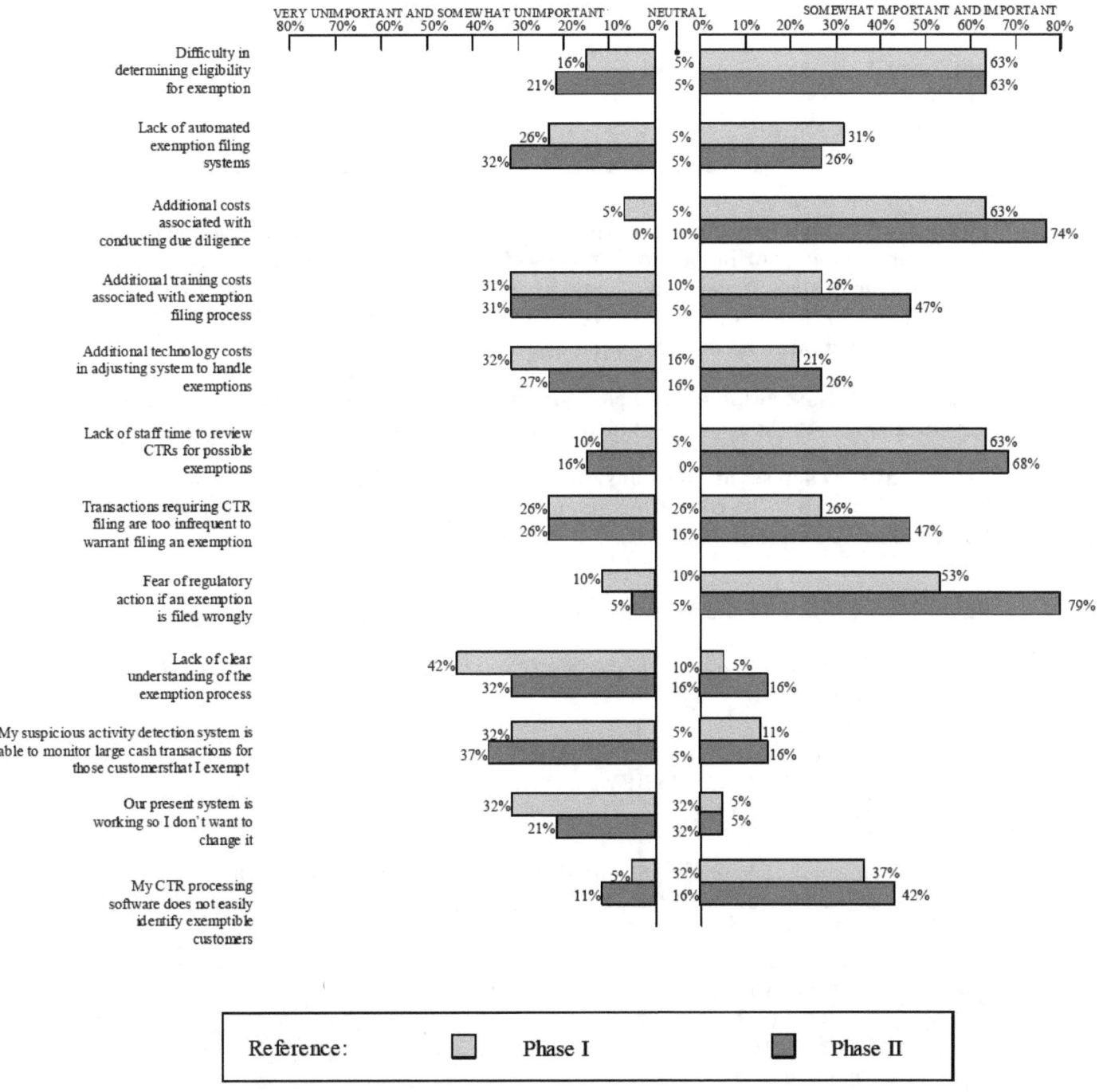

[22] "Do not know" percentages are not reflected in this graph.

FINCEN'S PATRIOT ACT SURVEY ON BANK SECRECY ACT (BSA) COSTS AND EXEMPTION PROCEDURES

RESPONDENT NAME: _____

TITLE:_____

INSTITUTION NAME: _____

E-MAIL ADDRESS: _____

Please answer each question as completely and accurately as possible, using information from your files or your institution's records if necessary. If you cannot complete the survey in one sitting or need to refer to documents to complete the survey, you may exit at any point. You can then resume the survey later at the question where you left off by re-entering your unique ID number and password.

Please answer the questions by clicking in the box next to the appropriate choices or typing in your answers in the space provided. We greatly value your opinions.

As you answer each set of questions, please use the next button below. Do not use the browser back and forward buttons to move through the survey. You can use your TAB button to move between the fields.

Information About Your Financial Institution

1. Which of the following best describes your financial institution? (CHECK ONE)
   Bank
   Savings & Loan
   Credit Union
   Other (PLEASE SPECIFY)
   None (GO TO END)

2. In which state or US territory does your financial institution have its primary U.S. headquarters? (CHECK ONE)
   Alabama (AL)
   Alaska (AK)
   Arizona (AZ)
   Arkansas (AR)
   California (CA)
   Colorado (CO)
   Connecticut (CT)
   Delaware (DE)
   District of Columbia (DC)

Florida (FL)
Georgia (GA)
Guam (GU)
Hawaii (HI)
Idaho (ID)
Illinois (IL)
Indiana (IN)
Iowa (IA)
Kansas (KS)
Kentucky (KY)
Louisiana (LA)
Maine (ME)
Maryland (MD)
Massachusetts (MA)
Michigan (MI)
Minnesota (MN)
Mississippi (MS)
Missouri (MO)
Montana (MT)
Nebraska (NE)
Nevada (NV)
New Hampshire (NH)
New Jersey (NJ)
New Mexico (NM)
New York (NY)
North Carolina (NC)
North Dakota (ND)
Northern Mariana Islands (MP)
Ohio (OH)
Oklahoma (OK)
Oregon (OR)
Pennsylvania (PA)
Puerto Rico (PR)
Rhode Island (RI)
South Carolina (SC)
South Dakota (SD)
Tennessee (TN)
Texas (TX)
Utah (UT)
Vermont (VT)
Virginia (VA)
Virgin Islands (VI)
Washington (WA)
West Virginia (WV)
Wisconsin (WI)
Wyoming (WY)

3. What are the total assets of your financial institution, including all subsidiaries? (CHECK ONE)
   Under $9.9 million
   $10 million to $49.9 million
   $50 million to $99.9 million
   $100 million to $499.9 million
   $500 million to $ 999.9 million
   $1 billion to $ 9.9 billion
   $10 billion to $74.9 billion
   $75 billion to $199.9 billion
   $200 billion to $499.9 billion
   $500 billion or more
   Not available

Currency Transaction Report Filing Process

4. Which of the following describes your role in filing Currency Transaction Reports (CTRs) for your financial institution? (CHECK ALL THAT APPLY)
   You have ultimate responsibility for the CTRs your institution files
   You make decisions related to the procedures and/or systems used in CTR filing
   You review the CTRs before they are submitted
   You personally submit CTRs
   You personally compile the information contained in the CTRs
   You are not directly involved in your institution's CTR filing process (IF 6, COMPLETE Q.5 THEN SKIP TO END. ALL OTHER RESPONSES GO TO Q6)

5. If you are not the appropriate respondent, please provide the name and e-mail address of the individual within your organization who is best qualified to complete this questionnaire.   (RECORD NAMES AND E-MAIL ADDRESSES. SKIP TO END.)

6. How many CTRs does your organization file annually?

7. From approximately how many different sites does your institution file CTRs? (CHECK ONE)
   1
   2 to 5
   6 to 10
   11 to 49
   50 to 99
   100 or more

8. From where are your institution's CTRs filed? (CHECK ALL THAT APPLY)
   Headquarters

Regional offices
Branch offices
Dedicated back-office
Main offices for different service lines (e.g., private banking, retail banking,
    correspondent banking, etc.)
Outsourced
Other (PLEASE SPECIFY)

9. How does your institution file its CTRs? (CHECK ONE)
    Electronically (using magnetic tape or diskette)
    Using paper forms created manually
    Combination of these

10. Approximately what is the average time to fill out, review and submit each CTR? (If you
    file both electronically and on paper, please enter the time for your primary filing
    mechanism.)
    Less than 15 minutes
    15 to 29 minutes
    30 to 44 minutes
    45 to 59 minutes
    1 hour up to 2 hours
    2 hours up to 3 hours
    More than 3 hours
    Do not know

Use of Exemptions

11. How many customers/members does the institution have? _____

12. How many customers did your institution exempt in 2001 and 2000? (INSERT
    NUMBER PER ROW)   2001   2000
    Number of Phase 1 exemption customers/members _____ _____
    Number of Phase 2 exemption customers/members _____ _____
    Do not know

13. Approximately what percentage of your customers fall into the following exemptible
    categories? (CHECK ONE PER ROW)
            0%   1-25% 26-50%   51-75%   76-99% 100% DK
    Eligible for Phase 1 exemption (bank, government entity or company listed on one of
    the major stock exchanges)
    Eligible for Phase 2 exemption (non-listed business and/or payroll
    customers/members)

14. To the best of your knowledge, what percentage of the CTRs that your institution filed in
    2001 was filed on exemptible customers? (CHECK ONE PER ROW)

0%   1-25% 26-50%   51-75%   76-99% 100% DK

Phase 1 exemption eligible (bank, government entity or company listed on one of the major stock exchanges)

Phase 2 exemption eligible (non-listed business and/or payroll customers/members)
Not eligible for exemption

15. What are your reasons for not exempting all eligible <u>Phase 1</u> customers/members?
(PLEASE RATE EACH OF THE REASONS LISTED BELOW AS: VERY UNIMPORTANT, SOMEWHAT UNIMPORTANT, NEUTRAL, SOMEWHAT IMPORTANT, VERY IMPORTANT, NOT APPLICABLE. CHECK ONE PER ROW)
     Difficulty in determining eligibility for exemption
     Lack of automated exemption filing systems
     Additional costs associated with conducting due diligence as part of continually reviewing exemption eligibility
     Additional training costs associated with exemption filing process
     Additional technology costs in adjusting system to handle exemptions
     Lack of staff time to review CTRs for possible exemptions
     Transactions requiring CTR filing are too infrequent to warrant filing an exemption
     Fear of regulatory action if an exemption is filed wrongly
     Lack of clear understanding of the exemption process
     My suspicious activity detection system is unable to monitor large cash transactions for those customers/entities that I exempt.
     Our present system is working so I don't want to change it
     My CTR processing software does not easily identify exemptible customers
     Other (SPECIFY)

16. What are your reasons for not exempting all eligible <u>Phase 2</u> customers/members?
(PLEASE RATE EACH OF THE REASONS LISTED BELOW AS: VERY UNIMPORTANT, SOMEWHAT UNIMPORTANT, NEUTRAL, SOMEWHAT IMPORTANT, VERY IMPORTANT, NOT APPLICABLE. CHECK ONE PER ROW)
     Difficulty in determining eligibility for exemption
     Lack of automated exemption filing systems
     Additional costs associated with conducting due diligence as part of continually reviewing exemption eligibility
     Additional training costs associated with exemption filing process
     Additional technology costs in adjusting system to handle exemptions
     Lack of staff time to review CTRs for possible exemptions
     Transactions requiring CTR filing are too infrequent to warrant filing an exemption
     Fear of regulatory action if an exemption is filed wrongly
     Lack of clear understanding of the exemption process
     My suspicious activity detection system is unable to monitor large cash transactions for those customers/entities that I exempt.
     Our present system is working so I don't want to change it
     My CTR processing software does not easily identify exemptible customers
     Other (SPECIFY)

17. Please indicate your level of agreement or disagreement with each of the following statements about the exemption process for CTRs. (CHECK ONE PER ROW)

(RESPONSE CHOICES ARE: DISAGREE STRONGLY, DISAGREE SLIGHTLY, NEITHER AGREE NOR DISAGREE, AGREE SLIGHTLY, AGREE STRONGLY, AND DON'T KNOW)

It is very difficult to determine which customers/members are eligible for an exemption

Exemption for Phase 1 and Phase 2 customers/members should be automatic, and the filing of CTRs for these classes of customers/members should be the exception

Frequent changes to the exemption rules means that we have to continually change our procedures to remain in compliance

It is less expensive to continually file CTRs than to file exemptions

We are concerned about regulatory action if an exemption is incorrectly filed

We do not have the staff to continually review customers/members' exemption status

We do not want to change a CTR filing system that is working

Too much personal judgment is involved in determining eligibility for Phase 2 exemptions

We do not fully understand the safe harbor rules for the exemption process

My institution's management encourages the utilization of exemptions

My institution's primary regulator encourages the utilization of exemptions

We would use the exemption process more if examiners criticized our failure to exempt appropriate customers/members

Evaluation of Possible Changes to CTR Filing Process

18. How would the following <u>changes in legislation</u> affect the level of burden on your institution of filing CTRs? (CHECK ONE PER ROW)

        Dramatically Decrease   Slightly Decrease   No Change

        Slightly Increase Dramatically Increase   Don't Know

Phase 1 exemptions are made mandatory

Phase 2 exemptions are made mandatory

The list of eligible, non-listed and /or payroll customers/members is expanded

The scope of the safe harbor provision from CTR violations is expanded/clarified (e.g., to specify that concepts of imputed knowledge will not apply to the non-filing of a CTR on an exempted customer)

Exempted transactions for non-listed businesses and payroll customers/members would not be subject to annual due diligence review

Reduce to 3 months (from 12 months) the amount of time required to observe a new account before applying for an exemption

Eliminate the obligation to determine whether an otherwise exemptible business is not subject to exemption because 50% of its gross revenues are derived from ineligible business activities

The $10,000 currency reporting threshold is increased

19. How would the following <u>changes in technology</u> affect the level of burden on your institution of making CTR filings (CHECK ONE PER ROW)
    Dramatically Decrease   Slightly Decrease   No Change
    Slightly Increase Dramatically Increase   Don't Know
    Better exemption processing technology is available
    Internet-based electronic exemption filing options were to become available
    Regulators regularly provide a list of exemptible Phase 1 customers/members that can be incorporated into your CTR processing software for screening exemptible customers/members

20. What else, if anything, could be done to encourage your institution to file exemptions for all qualifying customers/members? (PLEASE BE SPECIFIC) _____
    Do not know

<u>Suspicious Activity Reports</u>

21. How many SARs does your organization file annually? (IF Q21=0, THEN SKIP TO Q25)

22. From where are your institution's SARs filed? (CHECK ALL THAT APPLY)
    Headquarters
    Regional offices
    Branch offices
    Main offices for different service lines (e.g., private banking, retail banking, correspondent banking, etc.)
    Dedicated back-office
    Other (PLEASE SPECIFY)

23. Approximately what is the average time to review potentially suspicious activity, investigate the activity, and fill out and submit a SAR?
    Less than 1 hour
    1 to less than 2 hours
    2 to less than 5 hours
    5 to less than 8 hours
    1 to less than 2 days
    2 to less than 5 days
    1 to less than 2 weeks
    2 weeks to less than 4 weeks
    More than 4 weeks.
    Do not know

24. Of the suspicious activity that you investigate annually, please estimate the percentage that results in a SAR being filed?
    0 - 9%
    10 – 24%

25 – 49%
50 – 74%
Over 75%.
Do not know

25. How do you primarily monitor for suspicious activities? (SELECT ALL THAT APPLY)
Manual review of internal management information system (MIS) reports
An anti-money laundering or other suspicious activity detection system(s) purchased from a vendor
Internally developed suspicious activity detection systems
Manual identification of suspicious activities
Other (DESCRIBE)

Technology

26. (RESPOND ONLY IF Q9=2, THEN SKIP TO Q31). When, if ever, do you plan to automate or acquire automated tools to support your…

	CTR filing process?	Exemption filing process?	SAR Filing process
Within next year	☐	☐	☐
More than 1 year up to 2 years	☐	☐	☐
More than 2 years up to 3 years	☐	☐	☐
More than 3 years up to 5 years	☐	☐	☐
More than 5 years	☐	☐	☐
Never	☐	☐	☐
Do not know	☐	☐	☐
Not applicable	☐	☐	☐

27. Which of the following best describes the software used in your institution's CTR preparation and filing? (CHECK ONE)
System developed in-house or by contracted data processor/CUSO (Credit Union Service Organization)
System purchased from a software vendor: (PLEASE INCLUDE VENDOR'S NAME: _____)
Contractor with own system used
Combination of these

28. Which of the following exemption capabilities does the software that your institution uses for CTR filings have? (CHECK ALL THAT APPLY)
Identifies Phase 1 and Phase 2 exemption eligible organizations
Automatically creates exemption forms for exemption-eligible customers/members
Files exemption forms for Phase 1 exemptions
Files exemption forms for Phase 2 exemptions
Automatically filters out CTRs for exempted customers/members
None of these

29. What was the initial purchase/installation cost of the software your institution uses for... (CHECK ONE PER COLUMN)

	CTR Processing?	SAR Processing?
Less than $10,000	☐	☐
$10,000 to $49,999	☐	☐
$50,000 to $99,999	☐	☐
$100,000 to $249,999	☐	☐
$250,000 to $499,999	☐	☐
$500,000 or more	☐	☐
Not available	☐	☐
Not applicable	☐	☐

30. What are the annual licensing fees/upgrade costs for the software your institution uses for its... (CHECK ONE PER COLUMN)

	CTR Processing?	SAR Processing?
$0 to $999	☐	☐
$1,000 to $4,999	☐	☐
$5,000 to $9,999	☐	☐
$10,000 to $49,999	☐	☐
$50,000 to $99,999	☐	☐
$100,000 to $249,999	☐	☐
$250,000 to $499,999	☐	☐
$500,000 or more	☐	☐
Not available	☐	☐
Not applicable	☐	☐

31. How long would you expect it to take for your institution to develop software, modify existing systems or purchase new systems for meeting the following changes in exemption policy? (CHECK ONE BOX PER ROW)

CHOICES INCLUDE LESS THAN 6 MONTHS, 6 MONTHS UP TO 1 YEAR, 1 YEAR UP TO2 YEARS, 2 YEARS UP TO 3 YEARS, MORE THAN 3 YEARS, DON'T KNOW

Phase 1 exemptions are made mandatory

Phase 2 exemptions are made mandatory

The list of eligible, non-listed and /or payroll customers/members is expanded

The scope of the safe harbor provision from CTR violations is expanded/clarified (e.g., to specify that concepts of imputed knowledge will not apply to the non-filing of a CTR on an exempted customer)

Exempted transactions for non-listed businesses and payroll customers/members would not be subject to annual due diligence review

Reduce to 3 months (from 12 months) the amount of time required to observe a new account before applying for an exemption

Eliminate the obligation to determine whether an otherwise exemptible business is not subject to exemption because 50% of its gross revenues are derived from ineligible business activities

Regulators regularly provide a list of exemptible Phase 1 customers/members that can be incorporated into your CTR processing software for screening exemptible customers/members

Estimated Cost of Complying with the Bank Secrecy Act (BSA)

32. Does your institution capture actual costs of complying with the Bank Secrecy Act (BSA) and related laws and regulations as a distinct process? (NOTE: This would include **primary costs** such as labor and technology costs and <u>direct</u> administrative and material costs.)

     Yes
     No

33. What is the total annual cost to your institution of complying with the Bank Secrecy Act (BSA)? If your institution does not capture actual costs, please provide your best estimate of such costs. Again, please include **primary costs** such as labor and technology costs and <u>direct</u> administrative and material costs. (RECORD AMOUNT IN FULL DOLLARS. PLEASE GIVE A SINGLE FIGURE. RANGES ARE NOT ACCEPTED)

     $_____

     Do not know

34. We are trying to capture costs associated with complying with the Bank Secrecy Act regardless of where those costs reside within your organization. Therefore, please estimate the following cost components to the best of your ability realizing that in many cases your responses will necessarily be approximations. a) Select each job category below for which your organization has employees that dedicate a meaningful percentage of their time to BSA compliance efforts. (CHECK ALL THAT APPLY). b) Next, for each of these categories, please record how many people (Full Time Equivalents - FTEs) with BSA responsibilities your organization employs. c) Next, please estimate the average percentage of total work time spent by individuals in each category (FTEs) across CTR related activities, CTR exemption related activities, SAR related activities and other BSA activities.

Job category		FTEs	% of CTR Related Activities	% of CTR Exemption Related Activities	% of SAR Related Activities	% of Other BSA Activities
Branch staff	☐					
Branch management	☐					
Compliance department personnel	☐					
Legal staff/General Counsel	☐					

IT staff	☐					
Audit staff	☐					
Fraud prevention or other investigative staff	☐					
Training or HR staff	☐					
Corporate staff (not previously accounted for)	☐					
Administrative support	☐					
OTHER (Please specify) _____	☐					

35. What is the average, fully loaded compensation, including wages, benefits, bonuses and overtime, for the staff in each job category that has any involvement in the BSA compliance process? If multiple people in a job category spend time on BSA compliance activities, please provide an average compensation for that job category.
   (RECORD FULL DOLLAR FIGURE FOR EACH CATEGORY. GIVE SINGLE BEST ESTIMATE. RANGES CANNOT BE ACCEPTED)
   Branch staff
   Branch management
   Compliance department personnel
   Legal staff/General Counsel
   IT staff
   Audit staff
   Fraud prevention or other investigative staff
   Training or HR staff
   Corporate staff (not previously accounted for)
   Administrative support
   Other

36. (ASK ONLY IF CODE 3 OR 4 IS CIRCLED IN Q.27. IF ANY OTHER CODE GOTO Q37) How much does your institution spend annually on technology-related contractors who support your…

   (RECORD FULL DOLLAR AMOUNT. Please include programmers, IT support, off-site storage of files, etc.)
   CTR filing process? $ _____
   SAR processing? $_____

37. Please indicate the estimated amount of other non-technology direct expenses related to your institution's…
(RECORD A FULL DOLLAR FIGURE FOR EACH CATEGORY, INCLUDING 0 IF NONE OR NOT APPLICABLE. This includes the use of outside contractors, and services or materials used specifically to support the CTR filing process.)

	CTR filing process	SAR processing
Training	$_____	$_____

Legal support/services	$_____	$_____
Accounting/auditing services	$_____	$_____
Other (SPECIFY)	$_____	$_____

38. Approximately what percentages of your annual CTR filing costs are related to filing exemptions? (CHECK ONE)

0%
1-10%
11-20%
21-29%
30-39%
40-49%
50-59%
60-69%
70-79%
80-89%
90-99%
100%

39. Anything you would like to add?

_____

_____

_____

_____

THAT COMPLETES THE SURVEY. THANK YOU FOR YOUR TIME!